SNOW DAY

Reflections on the Practice of Ministry in the Northeast

Robert Allan Hill

University Press of America,® Inc.
Lanham · New York · Oxford

⊖™ The paper used in this publication meets the minimum
requirements of American National Standard for Information
Sciences—Permanence of Paper for Printed Library Materials,
ANSI Z39.48—1984

Contents

Preface

This little collection of occasional pieces is offered as a set of discussion openers ("ice-breakers") for those who are preparing for ministry in the Northeast. They are intended for those who know or will know the perils of skating on thin ice. Certainly the intended audience for this selection of provocations would begin with first and second year seminarians. Candidates for ministry and those considering ministry later in life might find some comfort here, too. In addition, one might hope that those who have weathered a few winters in the pulpit could find some catalytic inspiration here.

Chapter 1

Acoustical Avalanche: Toward a Cold Air Theology of Preaching

It is perhaps unfortunate that over time we in the frozen north have not allowed a powerfully central feature of our existence to teach us, more, about God. We have shoveled snow. We have groveled before storms. We have muffled our pleas for warmth. We have stifled our spouse's prayer, "take me to San Diego". We have trifled with the gruesome details of the weather channel. Shovel, grovel, muffle, stifle, trifle as we may, however, we have not fully considered the gracious presence of snow, and it is high time we did, thank you very much. James Sanders, OT teacher in Rochester and NYC, (before he moved to Los Angeles!) taught us to theologize first, then moralize. So before in moral indignation we lift another shovel, let us reason together about the gracious presence of snow.

a. Grace Prevenient

On the eastern end of Lake Ontario, whence cometh some wisdom, there is much snow and there are many snow days, in Watertown and Pulaski and Syracuse. Sandy Creek took on 54 inches of snow a few weeks ago, that town on Route 11, which we call "a little bit of heaven on Route 11".

That was a snow day, on the Tug Hill plateau. And a snow day is one day within in the Day of God on which all our strivings cease. A day that takes from our souls strain and stress and lets our ordered lives confess the beauty of God's peace. A day of preventive interruption, a day of personal reckoning, a day of cleansing health - a day of grace, within the one Day of God.

At 5 A. M. on a snow day, teachers pray for a day with family. Children implore the ivory goddess to wait upon their needs. Dads look forward to canceling class (though never church), calling in for messages, unbundling the toboggan, digging out that old 'tuke', and living, for once, in the interrupted preventive grace of God that says, flake by flake: *you are not God.*

One of the great anticipated moments of life in our home, a home of teachers and students over some generations, has been the rapt 5 A. M. televiewing of school closings, for which all fervently pray, as in other places, people light votive candles or clutch rosary beads or place prayer slips in temple walls. Please, oh please, please let this be a SNOW DAY. A Snow Day is a day of grace.

At judgment day you will not regret having spent a little time away from the office.

Come Sunday, Come Sundown, you will forget the many ordinary days, but the Snow day - the day of Dad's chili bean soup, the day of igloos cut with precision, the day of chipping the ice together from the roof, the day of grace - this you will take with you into God's presence, as a foretaste of heaven.

God knows, we need prevenient interruption. Otherwise, we think too much of our own doing, and too little of God.

> What counts in life is the love of God.
> What matters in existence is the grace of God.
> What needs doing most, God has already done.
> What costs most, God has given.
> What we can trust, God has offered.

So, says St. Paul, we do not preach ourselves - what we might do, what we might be, what we might accomplish - we preach Jesus Christ, and him crucified.

If we are not careful, if we do not accept the Snow Day, the day of prevenient grace, then we end up demanding Godly things of our spouse, expecting Godly achievement of ourselves, requiring Godly performance of our church, worshipping the creature and not the Creator, sculpting golden calves, and doing what most humans most of the time do - practicing idolatry.

There is one God and you are not God, nor is your husband, nor is your pastor, nor is your boss, nor is your parent, nor is your friend. Camus once said, rightly, that culture is meant mainly as a setting wherein we remind each other that none of us is God. "They shall understand how they correct one another, and that a limit, under the sun, shall curb them. Each tells the other that he is not God." Says Dorothy Day to Wall Street, "You are not God." Says Julian Bond to white America, "You are not God." Says Betty Friedan to the old boy network, "You are not God." Says the Republican congress to the Democratic President, "You are not God." And what does the President say? And in the new millenium, John Doe will remind women that they are not God either, and Jane Smith will remind children that they are not God either, and, if we can muster a little humility, we will all get by together, singing, "I am not God and you are not God, and we are not God together."

But it takes a Snow Day, the interrupting, preventing grace of God.

One Snow Day, fifteen years ago, when I was dyingly anxious to finish my Ph.D., resurrect Methodism, become financially independent, and win "father of the year" awards - all by the close of business that Tuesday--ASAP, I happened to stop, in the late afternoon, for a pastoral call, another important interruptive. An elderly botany professor, known for her guided tours of nature and popular courses at Syracuse University, and once seen in her mid-seventies, swinging from the limb of a sycamore tree which she partly climbed in order to make some now forgotten scholarly point, recited this little charmer to me on a brilliantly snowy day, as we drank tea in the later afternoon. Cold it was that day, and snowy, a day for limericks, and laughter and love:

> There once was a parson named Fiddle
> Who refused to accept a degree
> For he said, "'Tis enough to be Fiddle
> "Without being Fiddle, DD"

She included the poem, in a card, a few years later, at graduation, to make sure I did not miss the point. *Do you get it?*
Says the Snow to you and me, "Fiddle de de, Fiddle DD".

b. Grace Liberative

When St. Augustine in the fourth century was asked to teach his people about the Triune God, he offered this analogy: God the Father is like the Sun in the sky which lights and illumines and warms and gives life; God the Son is like the ray of sunlight that carries life and light and illumination and love to us; God the Spirit is like the touch of that sunray upon our cheek, which sustains and helps us, and which personally we feel.

But Augustine lived in sun and sand, like the young Camus. He preached with an African swing in his rhetoric: "bona bona, dona dona" - good gifts, good gifts. Had Augustine lived in Rochester, and not along the sunny beaches of North Africa, had he lived in the cold Northern climate, and not amid blue sky and ocean view and warmth in February - I mean, hello?, what kind of life is that? - had he your perspective on reality, he might rather have offered this analogy: God the Father is like a great cumulonimbus cloud moving over the earth, ready to cover and cleanse and beautify; God the Son is like snow, lovely snow, falling upon us to cover and cleanse and beautify; God the Spirit is like the touch of each unique flake upon our tongues and cheeks as we skate on the Manhattan rink, and feel personally a power that does cover and cleanse and beautify.

Think how the Scripture would be different if it had come from Upstate New York, and not the warm climate of Palestine...

And God separated the snow banks from the snow banks, those from under the firmament, from those over the firma-ment, and God called the firmament heaven. And there was evening and morning, a second day.

And Isaac took his huskies to drink by the frozen lake, and there met Rebecca, who came to break the ice and draw water. And he said, "Pray, put down your pick ax and let me drink from the icy flow".

And Pharaoh's daughter saw a sled come by downhill, in which there was wrapped in a snowsuit, a little boy, named Moses. Pharaoh's daughter took him home, and warmed him by the fire.

After the children of Israel had skated across the frozen Blue Sea, and Pharaoh's army was in close pursuit, the Lord God sent a heat wave that melted the ice and Pharaoh, and his chariots and his army plunged down into the briney deep.

By the icicles of Babylon we sat down and wept as our tormentors said to us, sing to us one of the songs of Zion.

Save me O God! For the avalanche has cascaded upon me...I have fallen into deep drifts and the snow sweeps over me.

Many snow drifts cannot bury love, neither can blizzards smother it.

Let Justice roll down like an avalanche, and righteousness as an unending blizzard.

I baptize you with snow, but One is coming who will baptize you with fire.

Except a man be born of snow and the spirit, he will not enter the kingdom of heaven.

God sends his snow upon the just and the unjust alike.

The wise man built his house upon the rock. The snow fell, and the blizzard came and the lake effect wind blew and beat upon that house, but it did not fall, because it was built upon the rock.

In the winter of 1966 there fell a tremendous snow. Our little village, 1100 feet above sea level on the northern edge of the Allegheny plateau, received a sudden interruption. Schools closed. Programs were cancelled. Trips were postponed. For two weeks the town just stopped in its tracks.   After a while, the supplies of milk and bread were running low. Danehy's market sported bare shelves and empty aisles.

There was a gracious and liberating pause. Looking back, I can see the stresses of that year - all of them resounding around the little Colgate campus - racial attacks by town kids, the first 13 undergraduate women living in the Colgate Inn, a neighbor's father teaching English and burning draft cards and losing his job for one or the other or both. Down came the snow, freeing us, freeing us from the role of Almighty God, and liberating our souls for an open future in the one Day of God.

That week, someone in Hamilton probably sat by the fire and read Josiah Royce: "Our world is the object of an all-inclusive and divine insight, which is thus the supreme reality."

Grace is not something you do, it is something that happens to you. Love is not something you own, it is something you receive and return.

When the 10 commandments proved not enough on their own - true and utterly on point as they are--God came to us, human to human, to free us from idolatry and settle a Snow Day on all our pride.

c. Grace Cleansing

Snow interrupts. Snow invades and liberates. Snow falls from on high, heaven sent. Snow falls as friendly presence, freeing its recipients of study, of work, of routine, and allowing, even forcing, a moment of conviviality, and community, and time and space for family and exercise and unexpected pause. Snow is unpredictable, uncontrollable, varied, dangerous, seasonal, cleansing, soothing, quieting and disquieting, cool, comforting, friendly and free. Snow falls upon us like grace, or grace falls upon us like snow.

We have some scouts in our churches, who are trustworthy, loyal, helpful, and so on.

Out in the snow, they have learned to respect one another and the God of Abraham, who made heaven and hearth, and who sends snow on the just and unjust alike.

Good troops go camping every month, including February. In a great snow, we went out into the Adirondacks to feel again the cold.comfort of the Day of God. That time - I may have been 13 - we stood in a circle before the ride home for some sort of ceremony. A few of us, warm again for the first time in three days, began running and throwing snowballs. It was innocent enough, I guess, except that one I threw hit a woman, a member of our church, right in the cheek. I remember just standing there, as the snow fell - light, bright, white- standing and waiting for the earth to swallow me so that I would not ever have to face her. Our scout leader I guess saw everything, that being his job to see everything. Because his hand, a snow covered glove, came gently onto my shoulder from behind, and he whispered, "Bob, why don't you just walk over and apologize to Mrs. Macaulay?" Which I did.

I guess they call that character education or value formation or something today. Probably there are millions of dollars spent on courses about it. You may be a teacher of this subject, I do not know. I suppose there is good in all this.

But I prefer, for formative impact, the snow covered glove, the kind but firm hand of a high school graduate farmer and carpenter, who watched and cared and whispered, like God watches and cares and whispers.

Our Scripture, a declaration of Grace, puts all this very simply, all this about grace preventive and grace liberative and grace cleansing: "He cured many".

And many cures He still.

I wonder about you. Will you accept a Snow Day if it is offered? Can you accept the white blanket of grace falling around your shoulders? Could you relax a bit and rely a bit on the Grace of God?

Here:

Would you accept the grace that gave you life?
That is Baptism.

Would you accept the grace that gives you the faith of
Jesus Christ?
That is Confirmation.

Would you accept the grace that gives you salvation?
That is Holy Communion.

Would you accept the grace that gives you Companionship?
That is Marriage.

Would you accept the grace that gives you forgiveness?
That is prayer and counsel.

Would you accept the grace that gives you a calling?
That is ordination.

Would you accept the grace that calls you home?
That is blessing in the extreme and at the last.

So we will recite with Paul:

It is no longer I who live
But Christ who lives in me
And the life I now live in the flesh
I live by the faith of the Son of God
Who loved me and gave himself up for me.

Chapter 2

The Significance Of Summer: A Contextual Theology of the Incarnation, Cross, and Resurrection (in the Writings of Philip Amerson, Douglas John Hall, and Barbara Brown Taylor)...or...A Visit to Chautauqua

An older idea about theological essays, one that some few of the more venerable among us will recognize even today, expected each to declare, however imperfectly, the whole counsel of God, the whole Gospel.

Our forebears, you could say, were on more intimate, more fraternal terms with death. So not a Sunday, not a single preachment, not a single essay, should pass, short of the entire, declared revelation of God. After all, who is to know what the week will bring?

Since the Second World War, though, our philosophies, religious and secular, have changed many times. Ideas drive lives. Our mental world has shrunk. We are postmodern, skeptical that anyone, anytime, anyway, anyhow, anywhere, could possibly state a full truth, let alone the full truth. And certainly not an itinerant, economically weak, culturally suspect preacher. Furthermore, our attention span has shrunk too. After two, now nearly three, TV generations, even Fosdick's twenty-two minutes stretches the sermon's hearing.

Nevertheless-

The Fourth of July is an uproariously full, kairotic time. The best weekend of the year, in my life - our anniversary, a daughter's birthday, the 10 mile freedom run, the great parade, a lake picnic, fireworks when it doesn't rain, recollections of various moves in the ministry all of which happen on this weekend - all experiences of a new birth of freedom. I love this holiday! It opens the summer.

Four years ago, we listened for the word of the God who keeps God's promises.

Three years ago, we traced together the outline of the mysterious dance of Christ with Culture.

Two years ago, you kindly received a sermon on the mound, and a celebration of Branch Rickey, Methodist Layman.

A year ago - as it happens, a far too prescient moment, I advocated a tactical retreat, a quiet slow summer, what Robert E. Lee rejected at Gettysburg.

This morning, with all the brash arrogance of our humanity, let us state the whole counsel of God, the whole of the Gospel. I summon as helpmates and witnesses three saintly living voices, simply to tell the full truth about God and about us. Each of these three is a hero of mine, a mentor, someone I admire. Oh, what I would give to spend a summer week with any one of them!

a. Incarnation

In the first place, our trust lies in the God who became incarnate, the Word who became flesh, born of woman, born under the law. God was in Christ, reconciling the world to Godself. Or, as Luther more trenchantly put it - "to seek God anywhere outside of Jesus is the devil."

It is good to be human! It is good to be alive! To eat, sleep, love, work, play, struggle, doubt, hurt, hope, and pray! "....a little lower than the angels!"

Phil Amerson, President of the Claremont School of Theology, consistently reminds me of this. You heard his voice in January, a preacher "happy in God" as Wesley would say, a big hearted, loving, bear of a man, who it happens, broke his arm last year. In Bloomington, Indiana, he was the pastor to coach Bobby Knight of basketball fame. Is there a truer measure of incarnate love than being pastor to Coach Knight, bless his evil being? I hear Phil and I recall Irenaeus, "the Glory of God is a human fully alive."

Phil wrote in the Oxford journal two years ago, "We are made with the Imago Dei, the image of God imprinted in our very genetic structure...We have the capacity for blessedness."

I wish I had more time this summer to learn from Phil about incarnation!

b. Crucifixion

In the second place, our trust lies in the God who sent God's Son to love us and give himself up for us. God takes the place of all who hurt – children, widows, the very poor, the crippled, the different, those at the dawn, twilight and in the shadow of life. The cross of Christ invades our hearts through compassion.

I recall every few days all year the Maundy Thursday service here. I hear the thud, thud, thud of the cross.

Where you most hurt, or will hurt, already God has been there with you, for you. In the Honduran barrion, in Kosovo, in the hospital, in the teeth of real failure and personal loss, at death, in what is hardest, the frightful hour of despondent ennui.

Now retired, Douglas John Hall, Canadian theologian of the cross, has for 30 years best-pronounced God's cruciform love. He has kept many of us from ignoring the superficiality, the falsity, the enslaving duplicity of our age that hurries, hurries, hurries us along until we drop from exhaustion, or emptiness.

He wrote, (*Lighten our Darkness*): "The church lives only as it is given over daily to participation in the death of the cross. Only as it is denied the glory it craves can it become the friend of those who can no longer pretend to glory...Only as it is brought again and again to the experience of its own limits will it be able to participate in the life of a whole age which has been brought face to face with the limits of human endeavor and the human species."

How I wish I had more free time together with my old teacher, Doug Hall, to learn from him about the crucifixion.

c. Resurrection

In the third place, our trust lies in the God whose love is stronger than death, who raised Jesus from the dead.

Heaven is here and now! Resurrection is the invasion *now* of selfishness by sensitivity. Resurrection is the interruption *now* of trauma by insight. Resurrection is the outbreak *now* of generosity in the face of self-aggrandizement.

There abides a Presence and a Purpose that you can trust with your very life.

The voice of Barbara Brown Taylor, Episcopal priest, has continued for many to evoke the raising of Jesus, in our time so alive to spirituality but so dead in spirit.

I hoped once to write a book titled *The Preaching Life.* A title borrowed from Annie Dillard's *The Writing Life.* One day I went into the bookstore and saw such a title, *The Preaching Life.* In it Taylor wrote, "The church's central task is an imaginative one. Everyone is born with imagination. Children are viruosi - they look at stars and see pinholes punched in dark cloth...They drape towels over their shoulders and become monarchs... Adults may agree that a comb is for hair, but children are not so limited. They know that a comb is also a musical instrument, a sifter for seashells, a backscratcher for dogs."

What I would give for a week to talk with her, to learn more from Barbara Brown Taylor about resurrection.

d. Conclusion

One Tuesday morning earlier this year, just before noon, the phone rang as I was leaving the office. My lunch appointment was at hand, my coat was on, and I was a man with a plan. I very nearly closed the door and let it ring.

Somehow, though, that didn't seem right. I crossed the beautiful office and took a call from Chautauqua - would I like to serve a week as Chaplain, August 1?

Immediately, with lunch getting cold, a host of oppositions arose - "I cannot come to the banquet don't bother me now..." I am busy. We have a full summer program at Asbury First...."Is that a 'no'" he asked?

That didn't seem right either. "Give me a day to think it over." Well, that afternoon my colleagues encouraged me, I swapped a preaching date for a future draft pick, and the next day the Chautauqua week was set. It felt right.

Without a call taken, a choice, postponed, an encouragement heard, an offer reconsidered, and a kindness accepted - like so much of life and our good future - this would not have happened.

Said the Wesleyans, "let the Spirit prompt". Said Tillich, "be open". Three weeks after the Chautauqua acceptance, a friend gave me a flier about this summer. Guess who is the morning preacher all through my week? *Barbara Brown Taylor!*

Four weeks or so after the Chautauqua acceptance, the institute sent out its full program. Guess who is the afternoon lecturer all through my week? *Douglas John Hall!*

Five weeks after the Chautauqua acceptance I took a phone call from a friend. Guess, which pastor will be vacationing there all through my week? *Philip E. Amerson!*

You know, we could all use a summer breather, and a little more Chautauqua acceptance, openness to prompting - incarnation, crucifixion, resurrection.

ON YOUR LIFE—

Can you live, from today, glad to be alive?
Will you accept, one dark day, God's cross closeness?
Do you listen, day by day for the voice of the resurrection?

Chapter 3

Icecapades: Three Things We Can Learn from Canada

A popular refrain in Montreal runs like this: "Canada could have had the best of three worlds: British government, American industry, and French culture; instead, Canada collected the worst of all three: French bureaucracy, British economics, and American culture!"

But don't you believe it. As that proverb's tangled contents and tone of wry self-criticism tell, Canada has a great deal to offer you and me. We can learn from our northern neighbors. This is part testimony and part admonition: Take a look at the Dominion of Canada. In particular, let me suggest three things that United Methodist's can bring across the border.

First, there is the Anglican Church of Canada. Its influence far exceeds that of its sister Protestant Episcopal Church in the Unite States. Though still statistically small, Canadian Anglicanism in one sense is the ecclesiastical leader of its land. We United Methodists-especially those out of the Methodist Episcopal tradition-need to hear the voice of the Church of England. After all, we are called to honor our father and mother; where would Methodism be without its Anglican mother? In this age when theological judgment is so frightfully difficult, the history and tradition and liturgy of this parent church have such to offer us. To take just one example: We Americans sometimes make much of religious experience. But there are some things that should not have to be learned from experience. The richness of our Anglican heritage can remind us of this.

Second, there is Doug Hall, teacher at McGill University in Montreal, former student of Paul Tillich, and author, His book *Lighten Our Darkness* sounds like a voice of realistic truth crying in pious wilderness.

For example:

The test of theological authenticity is whether we can present Jesus *as the crucified*. To be concrete: Can one perceive in the Jesus of this theology a man who knows the meaning of meaninglessness, the experience of negation, the anguish of hopelessness? Does he encounter the absurd, and with trembling? Would a man dare to confess to this Jesus his deepest anxieties, his most ultimate questions? Would such a Jesus comprehend the gnawing care of a generation of parents who live every day with the questions: Will my children be able to survive as human beings?...Will there be enough to eat? Will they be permitted to have children? Would he, the God-Man of this theology, be able to weep over the dead bodies of little children in Southeast Asia and Brazil, as he wept over his friend Lazarus?...Would he be able to agonize over the millions of other beings-not quite little-children, fetuses-for whom there was no place; and over the mothers...Could he share our doubt: doubt about God, about man, about life, about every absolute? Could he understand why we cling to expectations that are no longeraffirme-dor confirmed by experience, why we repress the most essential questions? Would such a Christ understand failure? Could he participate in *our* failure? Or is he eternally above all that?

> Douglas J. Hall, *Lighten Our Darkness: Toward an Indigenous Theology of the Cross*
> (Philadelphia: The Westminster Press, 1976), 211-212.

Third, there is the United Church. It was formed in 1925 as a union among Methodists, some Presbyterians, Congregationalists, and other Protestant groups. Today it is a church of some 2 million members (in a country of only 25 million), built out of a combination of Methodist and Presbyterian policy. It is not a church without problems. But for those of us who are still interested in walking a little further down the road toward ecumenism, the experience of the United Church in both its victories and defeats offers a glimpse of what our future might be like.

Canadian tourism commercials entice us to the natural, scenic, and cultural wonders of Canada, our neighbor to the north, "the world next door." United Methodist, I believe, have at least three other reasons for interest: Anglicanism, Doug Hall, the United Church. Take a look.

Chapter 4

Children of the North: Dear Old Boston

Introduction

The next time you are in Boston, take a moment to visit the Aquarium.

1. AH: This is dear old Boston, the home of the bean and the cod, where the Lowells will speak only to the Cabots, but the Cabots speak only to God. Boston, in so many ways the city of origin, the point of departure. Boston, birthplace of the republic: Haymarket Square, Old North Church, Bunker Hill, Old Ironsides. Boston, home to heroes: Paul Revere, John Hancock, Johnny Tremain. Boston, where in 1838 in the First Congregational Church heard a children's choir sing, "My Country tis of thee". On the Freedom Trail you can talk with "Ben Franklin" attired in the garb of 1780. On the subway you can stop at the Scully Square station and remember the man who never returned. Take the train to Fenway park and peer at the green monster. Try not to make the mistake of wearing a Yankees' hat. Walk through downtown and the flower gardens. Spend a minute along the old streets, and feel the freshness of a country being born, being formed, being built. Visit the children's science museum. Boston takes the world and makes it young again!

2. It may be that the best spot in this young city, this birthing room for freedom, is the Aquarium. Right on the port shoreline the city has built a magnificent structure, a several tiered tank. Coral has been transported from the Caribbean, and then also reproduced. Fish of dozens of colors, shapes, sizes swim in the blue green cylinder. Divers in fins,

wetsuits and air tanks maintain the giant manmade ocean tank. Stingrays swimming in a separate pool--you could touch them! And around and around the outside of the cylinder walk mesmerized children and adults, looking on the splendor of the Neptune's kingdom. There are six kinds of sharks in the Aquarium. The sand shark and others. At the top level you can watch them jump and swim. Boston returns one to the great ocean deep from which life at last emerged across the millennia. Boston takes the world and makes it young again!

3. On the day in which we visited the Aquarium, the place was mobbed, packed with kids and parents, classes and groups. The colors and shapes and sizes of the humans walking clockwise around the tank mimicked nicely the variety of fish swimming counterclockwise inside. I saw a little girl in dredlocks pressing her nose against the glass up toward the tank top, just as the sandshark swam by. Two Asian women photographed the coral. A boy screamed as he patted the stingray. There were maybe 3000 people inside the Aquarium. All of a sudden, the loudspeaker crackled. "Please be quiet, all of you." Soon the tall structure, full of children and parents, was nearly silent. The announcer continued, "I must regrettably report that a little boy is lost. He is three years old. He is wearing jeans and a white sweatshirt that says Boston College on the front. He has red hair. Please take a minute wherever you are and look toward the tank and then along the walkway." In a moment, you could feel the atmosphere in the building shift from lark to worry. Every parent's worst nightmare had hit. In the era of Kali Ann Poulton the tension around the tank was palpable. The thought that one child, even one, out for a Sunday of learning and play would disappear, or worse, held the gathered company on a tight leash.

4. In a single moment, the joy of the many had been overshadowed, darkly overshadowed, by the need of just one. All knew instinctively that there are no extra children, none to spare, not one to give up, to throw to the sharks. In that kind of dramatic moment, it is so very clear: every child is precious, every one dear.

b. *Children and Culture*

1. I have wondered a little since then, why the announcement so disturbed those of us who could see our own children. Of course you can think of many reasons. I believe however that one reason the announcement "child lost...white sweat shirt.." pierced the group that day is that we are dimly aware that there is a kind of warfare being waged against children in America today. Children suffer the effects of poverty most strongly. Children endure the effects of family demise most squarely. Children miss the care of physicians and dentists most keenly. Children feel the impact of bad diet most sharply. Children are too little, too weak, too powerless, too small in every way to watch out for themselves. Obvious enough. Children measure the depth of moral depression around us by measuring the amount of time, energy, commitment, and money within us, ready to be devoted to children.

2. This is not an easy time to grow up. Ask any elementary school teacher to compare her class with ones she remembers growing up. The difficulty arises not from a financial but from a cultural crisis.

3. The culture around us does not honor children, does not treat each little life as if it were "made in the image and likeness of God". Otherwise, we would not have the schools systems we have. Otherwise, we would not have the teen pregnancy we have. Otherwise, we would not need to have the number of surgical abortions we have. Otherwise, we would not have the vicious kinds of attacks on children which we now have.

4. There was a time when we actually believed that every child in this country needed, deserved a good education, and that we ourselves, in order to benefit from what Ortega called the "natural aristocracy" equally needed and deserved good, public education for all. We believed this, not in the sense that we said it, but in the sense that we gave ourselves to it. We gave our best middle class women to teaching, and many of our best lower middle and middle class men to teaching and administration. The best and brightest. We did not begrudge extra dollars spent for books and trips. We gave ourselves, as a people, as a culture, to education in a way that we no longer do.

5. Children in Asia today are raised, according to a recent report, with discipline, hard work and a passion for education. Discipline to reflect the ordering power of God. Work to reflect the creative energy of God. Education to reflect the life-giving newness of God's spirit. Children are made "in the image and likeness of God."

6. The cultural disdain for children all around us also enters the church. As a church, we have yet to achieve the kind of caring for children which we profess. The pious words of a recent "Durham Declaration" are ones we all share: "We believe that caring and providing for one another includes welcoming children into the family of the Church. As members of the Body of Christ, we know that children are gifts from God. In this we follow the example of our Lord, who, during his earthly ministry and in the face of opposition, welcomed children to his side. And we conform to the example of the early church, which, though living in the midst of a pagan empire that casually practiced abortion and abandoned children (usually to slavery, prostitution or death), helped to provide refuge for unwanted ones and their needy parents." (Didache: "you shall not murder a child by abortion or kill a newborn.") Good words. But anyone who has been around the church for very long knows that we do not completely practice what we preach, in this as in so many areas. We devote more language to love of children in church than we do actual time spent with children. Vacation Bible School is the bellwether for our commitment. Sunday School is a close second. Why is that when we have fellowship dinners we forget to provide childcare?

c. Children and Stewardship

1. Hear the Gospel, recipients of the gift of faith. Faith like yours really counts now. The lesson today speaks of contributing to the needs of the saints.

> Says Paul, you are children of the day!
> You are sunshine people!
> You are well fed at breakfast, scrubbed clean,
> carefully dressed, children with a purpose people!
> You have armor!
> You have a reason to get up in the morning!
> You have a reason to struggle on in the afternoon!

You have a reason to sleep soundly at night!
You have been touched by the Risen Christ!
You are God's people, God's movement for good,
God's protectors of children!
You are salt of earth and light of world!
You need not fear, but only watch and fight and
pray, and live rejoicing every day!

2. But, some will say, "I have no power. I am only a father at home watching my kids. I am only a teacher. I have no power. " You have the opportunity, today, to do something good for children, by supporting the ministry of your church.

Grace abounds in church: *Sunday School *Nursery School *Day Care *Girl Scouts *Children's Choirs *Counseling for Children *Confirmation *UMYF* Vacation Church School *UM Summer Camps *College Student Fellowship *Through children's time and time with children.

3. Where will the energy and time and money come from? Who will endow child care in the way someone endowed our medical school with a billion dollars for health care? If an ounce of prevention is worth a pound of cure, and there are 16 ounces in a pound, that's a 16 billion dollar endowment we ought to have invested in Rochester in healthy children!

4. One day this autumn, after a round of golf, two friends stopped at the home of a third to have supper. The host is a retired physician, a family doctor from the bygone days of "fee for service". Redolent with exercise and at ease in the company of friends, the doctor reflected on his life and work. An autumn evening, a twilight supper, a moment before winter-- this became an hour for thoughts in the autumn twilight of life, a moment before a great change of season.

He spoke about service and care. He ruminated regarding "the young doctors coming up". He unabashedly celebrated great-grandchildren, grandchildren, and children (both adopted and biological). A large family portrait hung on the living room wall. Mostly, though, this veteran of decades of stewardship campaigns talked about church. He reckoned.

"I try to tithe because in the church children get what they cannot get anywhere else. They catch a sense of wonder--wonder at the world, wonder at love, wonder before holiness. They see real kindness--kind people, kind ideas, kind words, kind works. Most of all, they learn about generosity--generosity in church that makes a world of difference. In the church seeds are planted: seeds of wonder, kindness, and generosity. I am happy to hope that my tithing has made a difference."

5. Friends, I challenge you this autumn to reckon with what matters most to you about the future. I challenge those who have never pledged to do so for the first time. I challenge those who have nominally pledged to stretch--to name a percentage of income to give away (to church or elsewhere) and then to commit. I challenge those who are ready to tithe. Some autumn, over supper, I believe you will be glad you did.

d. Conclusion

People know that there are no extra children, none to spare, not even one to throw to the sharks. When the need is clearly presented, the problem is almost solved. So it was on an August Sunday in dear old Boston, that after twenty minutes of looking and waiting, the tourists at the Boston Aquarium again heard the crackling loudspeaker, and again heard the announcer's voice, and at last heard the report: "the child is found! The lost is found! Several thousand people stared at one another and many fish and cheered instinctively, just as we will as a nation stand and cheer when every child across this great land has what she needs to make a life.

Chapter 5

The Art of Rebuilding: The Second Temple and a Second Look at Old Communities in Seven Moves

A. Rebuilding the Church: "Signs of Hope in Methodism"

I learned from George a most important lesson in practical theology: "Watch what the Holy Spirit is doing, and then follow." George had a certain style, a posture in life that makes him altogether memorable. He groused and slouched and cursed his way through months of meetings at the World Council of Churches in the days I knew him. He drew on a rare combination of Yale Divinity and the East Harlem Protestant Parish (a remarkable venture of a bygone era). When asked once why local churches flounder he barked, "Shoe leather! Those ministers don't spend the shoe leather, out on the street, mixing it up, making calls. Shoe leather!" He hired us to work on office things ("heat, light, and running water"), but mainly, I suspect, to plant seeds of good will for the WCC in the hearts of a few young people. He chose a few traditional liberals (me), I think as evangelism for the left. It didn't work. What I saw in Geneva made me a confirmed critic of church bureaucracy, religious politics, international ecuenism, and the Presbyterian Church. But George did win my heart, because he had so much heart of his own. In retrospect he was right, not only about shoe leather, but about the Spirit and the church. Spirit leads, church follows. Jurgen Moltmann spoke that summer about "giving account of the hope that is in you" (I Peter 3:15); George knew, lived, and preached the verse better. Hidden behind flat glasses, rumpled clothing, an ambitious porky belly, and a

seditious goatee, George murmured piously and accurately about the
Spirit: "I try to find out what the Spirit is doing, and then I join in."
    In concert with George, I want to notice here seven signs of hope in the
church: Spirit leads, church follows.

a. Bible

James Smart raised the question 30 years ago: Why is the Bible so
silent in the church? It goes unanswered still. The Bible has been
abused left and right. For the liberation theologian of whatever caste it
has become a pretext for progressive politics. For the traditional
churchman it remains a historical source book. For the new right, who
sadly take it more seriously than the rest of us, it functions, chiefly, as a
buttress for faith in an overly triumphant Jesus, an unstigmatized Lord.
Granted we all have our canon within the canon. Must the Word
continue to be so muffled?
    Here and there one sees a contrary phenomenon. One runs into the
Bible talking in the church. This *happens,* as William James taught that
truth happens, in the experience of life, lived in a profound way. The
Bible is not about Sinai, Jerusalem, and Ephesus. It is not about Jesus,
Paul and John. It is not about Israel, Judah, and a first century religious
movement later called Christianity. It is not about a collection of
religious and philosophical concepts. It is not about various courageous
men of faith from long ago. It is about *you*. The Bible is about your life,
as your life really is. The Bible tells the inner truth of your life.
    Gladys gave the scripture lesson of last Tuesday without knowing it.
She spoke of her isolation, her illness, and her discouragement. It is hard
to be tied to an oxygen tank when your heart is still young. She rambled
on about the election: "That Bush is a snake. I'd like to take a hatchet to
his face. I could put my finger right through his grin. He makes me
sick." She also spoke of her days alone. "I find myself, sometimes,
giggling and then laughing outright. I can't always say why." Then, after
40 minutes of monologue, she had come out down deep in the cavern of
living and met up with the Bible. "I just don't care, really, whether I live
or die." Genuinely now, and with real feeling: "Whether I live or die I
am the Lord's." (Romans 14:8). It is the Bible that provides the code of
living. We run into it down deep. It is a sign of real hope for our
denomination that people, intuitively, know this.

b. Preaching

Some ministers are daring again to think of themselves as preachers of the gospel. Not hawkers of the gospel, or salesmen of the church, or administrators, pastoral counselors, youth workers, community leaders, politicians, fundraisers, or the "glue" that holds the congregation together. Some few across the land have placed their lives in the service of an active, simple, local, friendly, piercing word of truth. This is not common. Nor is it the case with many who would want to claim this of themselves. It is not true simply of those who attend liturgy study groups, or work through exegetical outlines. It is true of a few who still believe that God can speak in a human voice, the humbler the better. We should not be looking for numbers here. The best movie I attended one year (Umberto Eco's "Name of the Rose") was so poorly attended that the theater almost refused to show it that night. Truth and popularity are not in direct proportion. (This is not an excuse for ill-prepared, boring, lifeless, stupid sermons.) Truth and popularity are often in inverse proportion.

When the preacher broods about his people, studies them, exegetes their lives, and then suddenly runs up against the Bible in them, he can begin to preach. One former research scientist left his laboratory nets a few years ago to follow Jesus to seminary. He survived this experience and has gone on to preach in four alarmingly poor little churches near Canada. I read his ordination exam sermon. It was about the strong and the weak, the strong who like to drink and brag of it, the weak who can't because of conscience. He preached hard and long about love among brothers, strong and weak. He referred, at some point, to Romans 14, which reading *was occurring* as he spoke in the life of his church. It was a long, careful, powerful, sober sermon which clearly was the word of God. It took a lot of work. It is a sign of real hope that preaching is again important to Methodism.

c. Visiting

The art of pastoral conversation has never been an easy one to master. As my first lay leader said, "I never met a minister who really knew how to listen." I find it encouraging that many younger ministers have reclaimed an almost lost talent for pastoral conversation as they visit in homes. One such minister, with no fanfare and no applause from the cabinet, has quietly spent seven years of ministry making a minimum of

30 visits each week. His churches have grown, modestly. His parishioners have grown, gracefully. He believes that his calling includes bearing witness, in the home, to Love's hatred of sin. Wesley taught that in only two activities was the preacher not wasting his time: preaching and visiting. The rest was and is a waste of time. We have become a denomination of meetings and meeting lovers. We are dying from it. Hope lies ahead, though, in the practice of the art of pastoral conversation.

d. Money

Our nation faces financial ruin. We have sold the birthright of independence for a mess of technological pottage. A church like ours, with such a bloated, superfluous bureaucratic superstructure, enters such time at great disadvantage. Since World War II we have milked our good churches and people to pay for programs, agencies, boards, executives, and "missions" that in hindsight are highly suspect. Religious pottage. With the national debt will come hard times for Methodism. There is hope here. The harsh economic winds should cleave through mountains of bureaucracy that otherwise would live on until the last trumpet. Our best dollars will no longer disappear into the remarkable entrails of 475 Riverside Drive. Our brightest ministers will no longer be assigned national staff positions. Our focus as conferences and as a denomination will no longer be on religious hokum. We won't be able to afford it.

e. Liberalism

Methodism has avoided the worst excesses of leftist religion. As a denomination, in my view, we are not happy about abortion. We still trust that men and women can, in prayer, learn to live together. We realize, in hindsight, that our exit from Vietnam meant 3 million Cambodian deaths. We understand that not only whites, but blacks as well, can be infected with racism. We are not willing to excuse every breach of personal discipline on the basis of Freudian, Marxist, or Nietzschean analysis. I don't think we're huffy about it, but we do tend to care enough still to challenge aberrant behavior. Here is hope: In the future, we will be able to present liberalism with integrity, at a time when liberal will mean "caring," not "permissive."

All this comes home in ordination. Episcopalians, Unitarians, Congregationalists, and other groups on the left have hurt themselves badly in the last 10 years in ordination, by refusing to ask about effectiveness. Wesley is still enough with us to whisper, "have they fruits?" Can he preach? Can she relate to people? Is he able to build churches? We need fewer, better ministers, and Boards of Ministry across the country are sensing this.

f. Students

There is an anger about the death of Methodist student ministry that is a harbinger of hope for rebirth of local church-related Wesley Foundations. Our lay people are leading the way.

The other day I walked across the Syracuse University Quad. A group of students had gathered at the quad's southeast corner. Pat Moody, English teacher and Methodist, was pointing toward a statue of Job. Below the statue were printed the words of Job 19:25, "I know that my redeemer lives." I overheard one blonde girl ask in a Long Island accent, "Look, can you give me a little background on this Job fellow? I don't know the story." On a sparking autumn afternoon, at the heart of the educational enterprise, within a stone's throw of a great chapel, a benchmark of the times. I walked over, catching the teacher's eye, and examined the pupil. "Of course you don't know the story. You are young, fair, white, rich, American, happy, and bound for success. That is, you are uneducated. Job is not meant for you, but for those with eyes to see and ears to hear. You are blind and deaf. Go home." Orange, amber, gold, red, brown, yellow: an afternoon of splendor and ignorance.

One out of 300 college students in America is infected with the AIDS virus. A student is more likely to get AIDS than a prison inmate. Why do we think that the front line, in the struggle with sin and death, is in Africa?

g. Long-Suffering

Strangely enough, Jesus still commands the allegiance of some of the best people around. In Methodism, these saints are found in almost every congregation. The quiet, strong, frugal, older Methodist lady, sitting along in the back pew. An usher of uncertain vintage, always in church except during hunting season. Two Trustees, who nurse the boiler along winter by winter. These and others like them are not the Morton

Downeys of life. They are not proud to be loud, and they don't particularly like people who are. They are, however, something like the salt of the earth. They have suffered for their Lord and his church, out of love.

Along with them stand aging clergymen who have given and suffered. They have, with grace, stepped aside to make way for the ambitious, the upwardly mobile, the pushy. In an age of permanent revolution, their moderation has not been highly valued, nor has it proved even to be an adequate defense against the excesses of others. They have been loyal and unaffirmed. The New Testament word for this passé fruit of the spirit is *upomone,* long-suffering. They are nearer the cross than many others. In their light we see light. They are a sign of real hope.

In 1988, on the surface, our church looks poor, weak, badly led, fragmented, adrift, wasteful, ineffective, off-course, over-organized, and creaking toward further decline in the next century. My friend, George, would growl, "Be sober, be watchful, the devil himself prowls around like a roaring lion seeking someone to devour." Sin abounds. *But: Grace overabounds.* George's idea of the Spirit gives us glimpses of hope. The Spirit visits us in the Bible, in preaching, in visiting, in money, in liberalism, in student ministry, and in long-suffering. This, it seems to me, is a ringing, divine endorsement of pastoral ministry.

B. Rebuilding the Temple: Ten Footnotes on Ezra and Nehemiah and the Return from Exile.

1. The crucial date in the history of Israel: 587bce.
2. How to read about the return: E: 1-4, N:1-7, 11-13, 9-10, E: 7-10, N: 8.
3. Ezra names resources needed to rebuild, E: 1-3: freedom, money, leaders, musicians, luck, horses and a firm foundation.
4. Various oppositions arise to rebuilding (E: 4). Can you list them?
5. To rebuild is to rebel (N: 1-2).
6. To rebuild is to restore, to repair, when "the people have a mind to work" (N:4:6).
7. The stories of rebuilding the temple and rebuilding the city are inextricably intertwined.

8. A remnant, though small, is sufficient (E: 9).
9. The walls are rebuilt one section at a time (N: 2).
10. THE JOY OF THE LORD IS YOUR STRENGTH! (N: 8:10).

C. Rebuilding the Small College: Five Footnotes from the Personal Faith and Public Life in the Northeast with *Dr. William Caruthers, President, Roberts Wesleyan.*

1. Roberts tries to bring the Christian perspective to class, requires study of OT\NT and chapel attendance. Conservative lifestyle, "old fashioned". Focus is on education for character. "We don't want faith destroyed as the result of a college education."
2. Life is not black and white, but lived in the gray. Leadership is more about being than doing. The character of the person who is leading is crucial. Faith, moral strength, self discipline. Servant leadership.
3. College is a niche institution, for parents who support traditional values. From 600 - 1500 students in 18 years.
4. Key programs:
   Organizational Management
   Council on Christian Colleges and Universities
   Full Campus Computerization
   Academic Quality
   Theological School
   Copyright of Management Program
   Hope to move to 2000 students
   Endowment form $200,000 to $12 Million
5. He spends his time primarily in four areas:
   Strategic Planning
   Fund Raising
   Community Relations
   Project Development

D. Rebuilding the City: Eleven Footnotes from the Personal Faith and Public Life in the Northeast with *Mr. Robert Doucette, esq., Urban Planner.*

1. Urban life brings people together. Rochester and Syracuse are similar, if you exchange salt for flour.
2. From the 1950's to the 1990's there have been major shifts in Northeastern urban life caused by movement to the suburbs, related to automobiles, inexpensive housing, cheap land, concerns about crime and schools. We are a very individualistic society.
3. Armory Square, Syracuse (slides) is a story of movement from blight to bloom: 38 new apartments, 2.5 miles from Carousel mall, retail shops that have been going for a decade, specialty and personal creative independent businesses.
4. We need to see cities in a long range historical context. The redevelopment of Armory Square took 14 years.
5. Our first impulse is to look out and see and say, "that's the way it is; that's the way it's going to be". But that's not necessarily true.
6. Cities have been changing for millenia. Rome in the 5th century went from a population of 1,000,000 to 50,000.
7. Change comes through: vision, passion, action, and commitment.
8. We forget: cities should be beautiful! We have lost a sense of common, public space. The last 2 generations lack experience with the city.
9. There are tried and true principles of urban design and we should stick with them.
10. Jane Jacobs is an important writer in this area.
11. Sometimes something has to die before there can be rebirth.

E. Rebuilding Urban Schools: Eight Footnotes from the Personal Faith and Public Life in the Northeast, *Dr. Daniel Lowengard Superintendent of Schools, Utica New York.*

1. 'Quick Fix" leadership does not deal well with complex problems that require complex solutions. We didn't get here overnight, and we won't leave that quickly either. Schools can be rebuilt, but not by one leader. Our first step is one of faith: "it can be done and

its worth doing".

2. Second, a regional approach is working in the Mohawk Valley. 75% of the children in Utica schools receive free lunch. The average Utica house is worth $53,000. Per capita income averages $12,000. But the spirit of cooperation in the Valley is prevailing. It is not enough to wait outside for a charismatic leader: people need to "jump in" for the outside.

3. Third, a leader needs an internal gyroscope to tell her or him when s/he is off track. Polls aren't enough. We get the leadership we deserve, and we have become impatient with leaders, rather than carefully cultivating the leadership we need. Schools are highly complex organizations that are resistant to change. Why do we open our schools only 10 months a year, from 8 am - 2 pm?

4. Fourth, often our definition of success is shortsighted. Success is longterm and comes from a combination of VISION, PASSION, and ACTION. Lou Pratt grew up in Utica. Today he is the CEO of Hewlett Packard. He said to the Mohawk Valley last year: "Quit the long looks and the rust belt mentality...I had to change my company due to competition from around the world. We spend a fraction of what we need to on technology. Upstate New York has resources: land, caring people, water, good workers."

5. Fifth, a good leader "sees the whole field". Principles are crucial.

6. Sixth, change comes from a combination of "external pressure and internal support". The leaders inside a system can change it if they have the necessary external pressure and encouragement.

7. Seventh, our biggest problem in staffing is the attitude, "it's not my job." Teachers are overworked and underpaid, but they also need to "see the whole field" and have a positive attitude: "there isn't anything that isn't my job if it helps kids."

8. Eighth, Utica is a city of 65,000. Only 3,000 vote in the school board elections. Schools employ 1600. The system changes one child, one school, one place at a time. IF YOU COULD DO ONE THING FOR ONE HOUR A WEEK, VOLUNTEER TO MENTOR IN A NEARBY SCHOOL. Kids succeed when they have caring adults in their lives.

Group discussion: What about competition? Isn't the reason that public schools fail that they don't have enough competition? Who are the school's customers: Parents? Students? Taxpayers? Are we really committed to educating every child in our poorest urban centers? How does faith energize us for our work? Do we have a moral compass that works? Are we one community?

F. Rebuilding the Church, Caveat: "The Dark Side of Church Growth".

Church growth, our most darling dream in Methodism just now, has its hard moments. These deserve more than the passing references they currently elicit. Church growth can hurt.

Several years ago I arrived at a dying city church. On the first Sunday 36 parishioners worshipped, all of whom were over 70 years of age, and almost all of whom have since died. In seven years the church had "taken in" (no pun intended) 238 new members. We lead two services of worship on Sunday, now, and we average 200 per Sunday. Our budget more than doubled in size, church program has mushroomed, the Sunday School has gone from 10 to 120, there are 15 in the youth group, the church now employs three ministers (myself and two part-time), the endowment has gone from $10,000 to $250,000, the church pays 100% of its apportionment, and we are all quite justly proud of our church.

However.

East of Eden it should not surprise I guess that there is a dark side to even the brightest moon. This growth costs and hurts, most of the cost and hurt are, as usual, born by the pastor and parsonage family. Consequently, they are too often unseen and unheard and so unquantified costs. Until the pastor has a heart attack. Prior to my heart attack, I offer these unbiased *(sic)* reflections.

1) The larger congregation is not as gracious as the smaller one was. The spirit of the tinier group more justly approximated the gospel. We are bigger but not more loving, more joyful, more peaceful, more patient, kinder, better, more faithful, gentler, more disciplined. We are less of these, and it is no one's fault, but it means pastoral pain.

2) New people come to the church, particularly when they come on confession of faith, because Jesus, they trust, will help them solve a problem, or problems. He does. He does so through the office

of the pastor and through the communion of the church. This means untold hours in which the pastor will counsel, listen to crabbing, supervise fist-fights, teach churchmanship, lay down the Methodist law on occasion, and generally relate himself and his family not to mature Christians but to immature Christians. This is hard work. It means angry meetings, butter late-night phone calls, uncharitable remarks, nasty notes. People may receive Baptism and Belief in a few moments, but learning to carry the cross takes longer, and means pastoral pain.

3) Consensus decreases as membership increases, and the bold moves and exciting decisions of the small group are heard to repeat in the large group. Someone's nose is always out of joint, and that means pastoral pain.

4) The first wave of new members can into an empty church. Among other more pious joys, these good folks also stayed because they received lots of attention, lots of airtime, lots of pastoral care, lots of time in the sun. As the church expands, they lose a good chunk of these things to others, and they see their own position weakened. "Someone else will do the children's time, and do it better. Someone else will have financial influence. When I came, I had all these to myself. Now I wonder whether I want to stay. The first new members start to put one foot in and one foot outside the door, and that means pastoral pain.

5) When we take in people, willy-nilly, and that is part of rapid church growth, we take in the potential arsonist. One verbal arsonist can, in two months, wreck two years worth of work. The Methodist hymnal and discipline do not ask us to require that people be "nice" as they come to Christ. May be they should. We have prospect lists, but we may also need suspect lists. Coarse language and rough behavior mean pastoral pain.

6) One generation returning to church, now ages 50 to 60, provides special opportunities for ministry *(sic)*. They have no abiding respect for their elders, no deep regard for ministerial authority, nothing but questions when political process is involved, and a generational chip on their shoulder the size of the Vietnam Memorial. It goes without saying that, at depth, they have very little in common with those now age 30 and those now age 60. It is an ugly wrinkle in time. This generation loves crisis. The church does not handle crisis too well. But: many recently

evangelized people come from this age group, whose children
are now ready to be confirmed. This means pastoral pain.

7) New people need a relationship with the pastor before they can
easily move on to skate on the full pond of church life. May be
this shouldn't be so, but it seems to be in my area of the world.
Like any relationship, this means social time together. Meals,
talks, coffee, movies. This takes an unbelievable amount of
time. The wear and tear on pastor and family are brutal. This
means pastoral pain.

If we are serious about growing, we will need to warn our people about
its underside, and prepare our preachers to insulate themselves against
the worst aspects of growth pain. We need the equivalent of Lamaz
training!

G. PostScript: Letter to Any Northeastern Bishop

Dear Bishop,

Welcome to the Northeast! We look forward to your leadership and
ministry among us, and would be glad to help in any particular ways you
may find useful during this transition time. Personally, as time permits,
I would love to have a meal with you and get better acquainted (and
scout out some good restaurants nearby for your present and future use).
Later in the fall, I will call your secretary and try to set a time.

I am writing this letter to record a somewhat strange vision daydream
I had this summer. I do not very often have this kind of experience. It
happened one morning during a walk.

In the daydream, you walked into my office across the lawn and said,
"Bob, what do think I should be doing as Bishop up here?" (How is that
for an arrogant daydream?!) I said:

"Our *identity* in Christ comes as we bear witness to the New Creation
(Gal 3:26-28), God's loving invasion of this world.

"Our *strategy* for living as witnesses to a new creation - for two
generations to come in this particular region anyway - has to be exclu-
sively the rebuilding of the foundations, the basic ministry of our
churches, which are now largely crumbling, weakened, and decayed.

"Our *mission*, through which the strategy can be achieved and the
identity matured, is solely *leadership development*. If we develop creative and loving lay and clergy leaders, our strategy and identity will
thrive. If not, we will continue to shrink, age, weaken and die.

"So: before you put anything in your calendar ask yourself, "Does this help develop leadership for the next two generations?" If so, go. If not, delegate. (How's that for unsolicited advice?!)"

Please pardon the blunt nature of this letter and the strangeness of the experience reported. Maybe it will be useful and thought-provoking, maybe not. In any case, I pray for your ministry here, wishing you all the very best, and watching for ways to assist.

Chapter 6

A Celebration of Northeastern Village Life: The Hamilton Chronicles

a. Language

I grew up in a little town that is steadily filled with a kind of twilight breeze. The Baptist church bells there ring every hour, sonorous and stately. It is a quiet place, forgotten except for its college. Most of the farms around it have grown up to brush again. There is not a lot of activity in the park, or on the main street. But it is a place where words matter. Growing up, our mailman was a Colgate graduate. So was the barber. Some of the farmers who lead and funded the church were, too. There is a gentle hum of words fitly spoken up and down the little lanes of Hamilton, and the day ends at twilight with a sense of rest and deep gratitude, especially for what has been heard and for what has been said. In that village twilight, the magic of language so enthralled me that I have been its permanent captive ever since.

b. Presence

An encounter with the Risen Christ, at any time, in an hour, within any season--His Presence filling our being--brings one to life.

For the preacher, at least, it is tempting to suppose that such encounters occur only in church, or only after proper indoctrination, or only as the consequence of adulthood or seminary training, or, even, only after proper enunciation and exposition of the Truth of Scripture. We can see and afffirm the partial truth conveyed in warnings such as these.

Life Herself, though, surges through our timidities, reminding us that God who made all things visible and invisible, that God incarnate in Jesus our Master, that God roving and hounding the earth by Holy Spirit, that God is not mocked and not limited and not put off and does not tarry forever. "Weeping may tarry for the night, but joy comes in the morning."

At this distance--150 miles and 30 years and a whole cultural cataclysm away--boyhood events, in retrospect, carry on their backs, like elephants transporting Hindu Kings, a kind of glory, Presence, Risen Christ among us. As, I look back, all that was happening and I hardly recognized it.

Kindness was speaking to me through the first Mrs. Shafer of my life, a bright brisk 6th grade teacher. Today she would be a minister or doctor or lawyer, probably, which would be great gain for the world but great loss for the sixth grade, where her astonishing gifts of imagination and sheer exuberance breathed spirit into flesh. Early in the morning I would haul out of bed, racing through breakfast, sneakers sticking in the spring mud, pounding past Fraternity Row to be the first to school, often before the doors were unlocked. I would walk around outside, until the hour struck, then find my class, my desk with its little ink well and carvings from generations of Emerald Knights before, and talk with Her before class. That spring She read to us the Hobbit, to start each day. · She strode the middle aisle, pacing, reading, smiling. When hard news came later that month I was ill for two weeks, pajamas and ginger ale. She came up the path and sat and read, after school, so that I would not miss the story, I would know how far Bilbo Baggins and Gandalf had gone. She coaxed me back to life, after the bad news came, reading and talking. She told me Nathan Terrell, whose father was a pacifist philosopher at Colgate, wanted to debate me in class over my support of the War in Vietnam. 11 year olds solving the world's problems. All energy, all spunk, all heart and tight frame, my first Mrs. Shafer quickened me with Kindness, early in the morning.

Joy met us, strangely, all around in that college town. Colgate was all men in those years, except by apocalyptic invasion, now and then, during what I remember were called "Party Weekends". Young women from Cazenovia College would come for two days and be billeted in homes through the town. Looking back, I suppose there was some financial arrangement, but the young women who stayed with us became family. They were usually dating the pre-seminary students who helped in the church. They brought gifts and beauty and, now I see, windows into another world. They would stay in my room--I thrown to sleep on the couch--and for days later the room would be filled with scents and touches foreign to our parsonage existence. Early in the morning, before breakfast, my sisters and I would pad into the converted guest room to watch, with awe, the makeup process. These were novel, unknown magics, conjured on a forlorn bureau whose drawers held baseball cards and yo-yo's. Later, when the dark report came, packing that bureau hurt. There, before the altar of Venus, the priestess would work her sacramental magic. Lipstick, rouge, perfume, hairspray--magics all. My sisters (and I too) sat like aboriginals at last brought to court, like the Indians Columbus took back to Europe, like the Shawnee seeing rifles for the first time, like Dr. Livingston's Africans wondering at his medicines, like Dorothy and friends before Oz the great and powerful. Every movement was studied. We sat, in a row, mesmerized while the Goddess laughed and primmed and adjusted from glory to glory. Once She, Joy Herself, took my sister and sat her atop the battered bureau. A frightening, holy second. The Priestess Goddess, bowing to Venus, then took her supplicant and applied the same magics--lipstick and rouge and perfume and hairspray, to our Parents' horror. Did not Paul write, "women should adorn themselves modestly and sensibly in seemly apparel, not with braided hair or gold or pearls or costly attire but by good deeds, as befits women who profess religion" (1Timothy 2:9)? Joy, strange happy joy, early in the morning.

Patience, too, wafted Her way around the streets and cowpaths and alleyways of childhood. Early in the morning, the phone rang. "Grandma died". I learned later that she had been suffering in a far--off city hospital. She had been a nurse, there. Her doctor, her boss for many years, watched her into suffering illness. Her last night, lungs collapsing, she gasped and gasped, writhing. "Isn't there something you can do for her doctor?" "Give me a minute alone with her". 1963. She peacefully died. I saw my father cry, for the first time. Early in the morning, the phone rang. "You have a brother." Sisters are fine. But a brother! Lots of noise at night in the small house, with now four kids. Crying and walking, feeding and bathing. Early in the morning, the phone rang. "The Bishop would like to see you." Who could know the meaning of such a phrase? Early in the morning, the phone rang. "Send him up to campus for the summer science program". Early in the morning, the phone rang. "Goodbye".

Gentleness Herself ambled about the land, in those days. Ice skating, sleds, swimming lessons, autumn, the Baptist bells hour by hour and loud and deep, early in the morning. After breakfast, that spring, She, Gentle Grace, sat with me on the back steps. The words hardly landed, caught as I was in the Eastertide reverie of boyhood. From where we sat I could spot two windows through which I had flown, launched, catapulted balls. Sons break, fathers repair, the world turns. I could see a half finished go-cart, no wheels. I could look at the neighbors' garden, which I had also tilled for fun--such is youth. Across the street lived the feared Russian professor, next door to the feared TKE's, alongside the feared empty, possibly haunted, house. I could see the evidence of unreflective, free life, naive, unaware, redolent with happiness, responsive. Gently She spoke, but again I could not hear or believe or intuit. "We are moving in June." "Bob, we are going to move in June after Conference." I have not felt such grief or cried such tears, except when my own son heard the same words at the same age thirty years later. We had not needed privacy, before, in which to speak. Somehow I should have known that a back porch talk meant dark news. Early, early, too early to gather the friends, and attempt to puzzle through the meaning of such disaster.

Christ has died. Christ is Risen. Christ will come again.

Recall Wilder's Emily Webb returning from the dead... *She asks, just once, to return to Grovers' Corners, to see and hear and taste and touch and feel. "Choose the least important day in your life. It will be important enough." She picks her 12th birthday, at dawn, early in the morning.*

Three days snow, in Grover's Corners. Main Street, the drug store. Mr. Webb coming home on the night train from Hamilton College. Howie Newsome, the policeman. Mrs. Webb ("how young she looks! I didn't know Mama was ever that young"). 10 below zero.

> *I can't find my blue ribbon.*
> *Open your eyes dear. I laid it out for you.*
> *If it were a snake it would bite you.*

The milkman arrives. Mr. Webb kisses Mrs. Webb. Don't forget Charles it's Emily's birthday.

I've got something right here. Where is she? Where's my birthday girl?

Breakfast, early in the morning, in Vermont. A very happy birthday to you. There are some surprises on the kitchen table. But birthday or no birthday I want you to eat your breakfast good and slow.

I want you to grow up and be a good, strong girl.
That blue paper is from your Aunt Carrie.
And I reckon you can guess who brought the post-card album
I found it on the doorstep when I brought in the milk--George
Gibbs.
Chew that bacon good and slow. It'll keep you warm on a cold
day.

O Mama, look at me one minute as though you really saw me. Mama
14 years have gone by. I'm dead. You're a grandmother Mama. I
married George Gibbs. Wally's dead too. His appendix burst on a
camping trip to North Conway. We felt just terrible about it--don't you
remember? But, just for a moment now we're all together, Mama. Just
for a moment we're happy. LET'S LOOK AT ONE ANOTHER.
So all that was going on and we never noticed. Grover's Corners.
Mama and Papa. Clock's ticking. Sunflowers. Food and coffee. New
ironed dresses and hot baths. Sleeping and waking up. Earth! You are
too wonderful for anybody to realize you!...

Recall the Spiritual gospel. On the first day of the week Mary
Magdalene came to the tomb early in the morning. She found as we find
every morning of our lives that Christ is Risen.

She called Peter and John and they found what we find every morning
of our lives that Christ is Risen.

Mary wept and then heard as we hear every morning of our lives, Jesus
calling our names.

With Mary, early in the morning, may we learn also to do as she did
that day every morning of our lives: honestly to tell what we have seen of
the Lord.

c. Spiritual Geography: Coming Home

Once, sometimes twice, each summer I tag along with the family for
their weekly, Saturday visit to the Hamilton farmer's market. Rain or
shine, come Saturday, those with treasures to trade meet up with those
with a desire to deal, on the old Hamilton green. The green sits, in the
New England style, right in the center of town, splashing up against the
old bandstand and the various War memorials and the fountain. Step-
ping between hagglers and shopaholics, men and women, there in the
summer is America, there in the summer is life. "In Him was life, and the
life was the light of all people".

Your nose will guide you. Racks of flowers offer a sweet scent. Fried dough commands interest from nose and throat and stomach, too. It seems like you can smell the baked bread, even through the wrapper. And as the harvest tide rolls in, week by week, the harvest table fills: with cucumbers and corn and tomatoes and beans.

Everything you never knew you needed is on display: lawn ornaments, shepherds crooks, homemade games devised from nuts and bolts, quilts, books, tickets to the next Methodist church apportionment barbecue.

I bought a used futon. My dad asked what I had bought at the market. "A futon", I said. "Why would you buy one cruton?", he scolded. "I didn't buy a cruton", I remonstrated. "But you just said you did", he asserted. "Not a cruton, but a futon I bought", said I. "A what?" (My dad has a little hearing impediment, and very definite ideas). "A futon". "What in the world is a futon?", he cajoled. On vacation, playing, I replied, "Oh, it's a little piece of bread, toasted, that you put on salad". "You did never make sense", he said, but he smiled, and I did too. Sometimes it's not the words, but the music that matters. (Yes, thank you, choir!)

Around the square stand sentinel the buildings of the town. Town Hall, with a widow's walk, is built on the edge of the old Chenango Canal, now Route 12. The Library, where Mrs. Howe is still the librarian, is as much the town center as ever. The Colgate Inn, 1877, is continually remolded, continually reformed, continually rebuilt, like the Body of Christ, the church. A post office. Several ante-bellum homes. The Smith Building, for commerce, dated 1848. The Burgess funeral parlor, with two American flags flying from the porch ends. The town has kept its identity, its character, for over a century. My brother, who now lives in Virginia, says this of Upstate New York: "I come up each year and I feel that nature is reclaiming what history built. Fewer farms, more woods. Fewer people, more space. Fewer cars, more overgrowth." The Hamilton green, holding its farmer's market, remains though,resisting the forest primeval, the downturned economy, and even theimmigration of yuppies, muppies, dinks, buppies and other folk to Virginia.

Two churches eye each other with sibling jealousy and affection. The Baptist Church (1796) and the Methodist Church (1808). I would rather say the Methodist Church and the Baptist Church, but Hamilton, like Rochester, is an old regular Baptist town. I grew up between the sister churches, on the green. There, with gentleness and kindness, we learned a creed like that of Romans 12, the Pauline 13, "Let love be genuine..."

So every farmer's market is a homecoming, an emotional bath. I careen around the square, bumbing into shoppers, lurching from stall to stall, wild-eyed, teary, mumbling, gesticulating, engrossed in conversations from 30 years ago. I imagine the prodigal one had the same decades old talks, as he walked home. The people on the green step aside, making way for a six-foot demented native son. My heart spills out frightening memories, like the fountain at square center. I am red-faced, weeping and crazed, coming home. I think I am bad for business.

At the bandstand you find the harvest table. I stand there, but I do not see the corn and tomatoes. Instead, before me, *in the mind's eye,* is my childhood friend, Jill Hance. It is the summer of 1965. We are nearly eleven. I have not seen her all summer, but we have sat in elementary desks together so long--Fragola, Gordon, Hance, Hill, Jones--alphabet order, we are friends. Here she is, bespectacled, on her red Schwinn, smiling. "The Giants traded Cepeda for Sadeki.." "Orlando Cepeda for..who?" But I am stunned. Something has befallen her over the summer. She is--bigger. She is--taller. She is--fuller. If she were a color it would be pink. If she were a star, it would be Venus. It she were a food it would be cream. If she were an adjective it would be round. Something has happened.

"Three things are too wonderful for me;
four, I do not understand:
the way of an eagle in the sky,
the way of a serpent on a rock,
the way of a ship on the high seas,
and the way of a man with a woman." (Proverbs 30)

(I think the church better find its tongue and voice again when it comes to simple human maturation and sexuality. I think we could at least come up to the Biblical level. If healthy speech is silenced, only sickness will sound out.) *Meanwhile, back on the green,* I begin to shout, "I do not understand. No one told me it would be just like this. She is so personal, so different, so lovely (like the (1) Gospel of John, and like real ministry anywhere, anytime, I point out now). No one warned me! She is so ... round!" I reach out wildly, motioning to Jill...but the farmer is holding his produce, guarding his tomatoes. "Yes it is round. But what is wrong with you? Do you want to buy something?" I hurry on. My children disown me.

Meanwhile the Methodist ladies are hawking chicken tickets. I walk over. We chat. I fumble for a bill. But then I look up, and behind them, across the street, *in the mind's eye,* suddenly I see a blue Ford Mustang convertible, with a white interior. There is Miss Lenhart, our fifth grade teacher. (Robin Williams in "Jack" is surely not the only kid to fall in love with a fifth grade teacher.) We stand by the car, getting ready to ride. She laughs, tosses her blond and hair, puts on sunglasses. I want to tell her something, about how all that careful teaching made a difference in my life, something about insight and imagination and inspiration (the marrow, I realize, of the (2) Gospel of John). I reach out, and begin speaking about the *Hobbit...* when you read us the *Hobbit...*but *meanwhile, back on the Green,* the Methodist chicken lady says, "Hobbit--no ticket, here is your ticket. I stumble away. I hurry on. My wife disowns me.

At the south end of the green, across from the Baptist steeple, I see the old funeral home. The Baptist chimes rings the hour. Gong. *In the mind's eye,* I listen from bed at night. I grew up under those chimes, just like kids in Rochester grow up under ours. Their sonorous thudding song marked my life. Time. The hour is coming and now is, the (3) Gospel of John reminds us. Chicken pox. Gong. The first mud of spring. Gong. Hot, too hot to sleep summer hot. Gong. The bells ring out gently at night, bringing harmony to the other night sounds of a lifetime. TKE house parties. Gong. An early milk truck, crunching snow. Gong. The sounds from the bandstands on Thursdays, too many flutes, too few brass. Colgate graduation, hundreds of men circling the pond at night, singing the Alma Mater, torches lit. A lifted torch, a lifted hymn, a lifted soul: young, young life!

Meanwhile, back on the green, it is noon. The market is closing down.

A woman selling quilts stands up to go. I see behind her the funeral home steps, six wide steps freshly painted battleship gray. The flags flap, like sisters talking on the porch. I look at the quilts, then I look up. *In the mind's eye* it is a cold spring day. I have come from a scout meeting. There,under the gray sky and above the six gray steps of the funeral parlor, I see a casket wrapped in yet a third flag. Some sort of military group stands along the walk. There are two parents, I know them vaguely, like everyone knows everyone in a small town (no one uses turn signals in a small town, because everyone knows where everyone is going anyway). They walk behind the casket. Their son graduated the year before, an Emerald Knight, as the graduates of Hamilton Central are known, class of 1965. I can see him, last fall, a friend of David Risley's, talking to a girl at the football game. Now he is in a long box. "I don't understand. I don't understand. I don't understand." (We have shouted the same this summer for many who have left us too soon.) Like the (4) Gospel of John, concerned for abundant life. *But meanwhile, back on the green,* the quilt woman is grabbing her merchandise back, and I am shouting and weeping, and she says, "I'm sorry if you don't understand, the price is fixed. $80.00." "Too high a price", I murmur, thinking not of the quilt, but of the boxed Emerald Knight, dead at 19, carried down the same gray steps by handsome uniformed friends. I hurry on. My family disowns me.

You can see why I seldom go home. I'm bad for business at the farmer's market. And there's only so much a family can take. I admit to some hyperbole, today, a manner of speech Jesus also adorned and beautified, in his parables, and in those told after his resurrection, by his friends, like this gnostic story of the prodigal son. I exaggerate a little, to make a single point: Coming home is painfully, terribly hard. It means seeing two worlds at once, now and then. It means hearing two voices at once, human and divine. It means both the chaos of the market and the ghosts of meaning hidden there. It means both the hubbub of worship and the meaning hidden here, for you, behind pew and hymnal and window and altar. Coming home means seeing light in darkness and meaning in life. It means tears, madness, looking foolish, and the occasional accident. Coming home means an experience of God, from within. Coming home means an experience of God, from beyond. I invite you to come home in faith this year.

I do not lightly invite you home. In fact, bad as this may sound for religious business, it may be more timely for you to stay away. You can stay away, out with the husks, in different guises: by playing golf on Sunday, ruthless and honest; or by getting heavily involved in church activity in order to avoid the hurt of real faith (a lot of hiding out there is in church--especially in committees--easier to fax and figure and finagle than to face your own death, upcoming); or, you can even enter the ministry, and postpone a real experience of God in the name of the service of God. I know.

But this year, I am coming home. I am going to walk through the village green of faith. I am even going to return to the fearful town of my own first faith love, the Gospel of John: to see its houses and stories and people, but also its ghosts and angels and spirits. It scares me. I sure would like some company. Maybe you're ready to come along. I'll try not to embarrass either of us too much, by shouting or hysteria.

Let us speak from the heart this year. Let us honor life by taking of our bodies this year. Let us, in Paul Ricouer's phrase, "find meaning through a second naivete". Let's come home together, to an experience of genuine love.

I'm going out to clean the pasture spring;
I'll only stop to rake the leaves away
(And to watch the water clear, I may):
I shan't be gone long--You come too.

I'm going out to fetch the little calf
That's standing by the mother. It's so young
It totters when she licks it with her tongue.
I shan't be gone long--You come too.

d. Deneoument

The end comes too quickly, for what is real and good. We grew up outside in the little lanes of our village, especially when the weather swung around warm, as it does in just a few days in the Northeast. The iron matriarchy of Hamilton decreed that the day's own trouble ended, come evening, when the streetlights came on. You may have been in an extra inning game, with the bases loaded and full count. Too bad, the street lights came on. You may have marched hundreds of little Asian yellow and German blue and American green soldiers all the way into a sandlot battle of the bulge, with just a thrust left for victory. Too bad, the street lights are on, the battle is over. That town even had a soda fountain, so that in later years, when bat and ball gave way to other interests, there was a place to watch the opposite gender becoming the opposite gender and to be lost in wonder, love and praise. You may have just squeezed in next to someone, when, the word passed, the street lights are on. Too bad. You lose. Cursed street lights.

Spring brings departures. People say goodbye in the springtime. At funerals. In office departures. In moves. At weddings. At graduations. In itinerant appointments. In memorials. In confirmation. There is a great deal of ending in the spring, for such a season of growth. It is a time of farewell, of streetlights closing the day. Through such trials, love persists.

One spring afternoon, I was invited at age 11 to a back step conversation. The contralto persistent voice of the backstep is not poorer or richer than a baritone public voice, but it is other. In this voice, there was that day an unusual uncertainty. There was a wandering, a certain wandering around robin hood's barn. I was frankly lost and bored, until new vocabulary reared its ugly head. There were new nouns sprinkling the afternoon: bishop, appointment, annual, new town, calling. There were verbs descending too: change, move, itinerate. Now I listened more closely, because I could feel an ending, a frightening ending, a departure at hand. I had to listen carefully too because I couldn't see—you know how in an emotional conversation sometimes a watery film comes down over your eyes and nose and you can't see well. So I listened, at the end, to a persistent loving contralto voice, not better or worse than the pulpit baritone, but somehow, that day, much more powerful.

We are going to move. It will be hard. But you will be fine. You will see. You will make new friends. You will have new chances. You will grow up like you never could here. Trust me. It will be alright. And I will be right there with you. We all will be together. And you can come back and visit. It is all going to work out just right.

Love, real and good, eschews insistence and practices persistence.

Can we become a persistent people?

Chapter 7

Student Ministry: How to Be Happy in College

In the Northeast, we specialize in college life. Have we suggested how one can become happy in school?

The only Scriptural account we have of Jesus' growth and boyhood is located in Luke 2:41-52. Only here does the Gospel allow us a glimpse of Jesus growing up. In this one picture of our Lord's maturation, we find him at the feet of the great teachers of his time. This is Jesus as a student.

Later ages, and later writings, did not resist the urge to imagine Jesus in his boyhood, clever, magical, boy deity, able to make birds from stones and animals from the very dirt at his feet. But the Gospel, in which we stand, refrains from wilder speculation. Only here, just for a moment, does the writer relent and, in the reading meant for the Sunday after Christmas, show us the student Jesus. He who was to call disciples, now himself, just this once, is a disciple too.

What good news this is for students near and far, and for grandparents and parents and teachers and all who labor and are heavy laden in the educational projects of our time! College is a nice idea, but very expensive. As he blessed weddings in Cana and healers in Bethany, so now Jesus, by his presence and practice, blesses students.

Jesus is our transforming friend. We have gathered, after already much church this week, to pray and listen for grace, because of Jesus, our transforming friend. We bear witness, today, that Jesus has transformed our life, made us happier and better people than otherwise we would have been without him. How we hope that young people will ex-

perience his power and love, in their own way and time, in college!
it may be, brings the preacher to the point of having the temerity to offer
any advice of any kind on anything. To know Christ is to know His
benefits, said the reformers. Counting those benefits may be one of the
joys of aging.

Men will tell you that aging can be bittersweet.

Like the day after engagement when you are told about registering for
china and appliances for wedding gifts. You feel older. But I just
wanted to get married! What is all this merchandizing?

Or when you turn thirty, from twenty nine. A day that will live in
infamy, a day of darkness and not of light. Who may abide the day and
its coming? It is like a refiner's fire. Illness descends.

Like the decision to buy a van, and to sell a convertible. The shift from
sports car to van or station wagon - need I say more? Is there a surer
measure of aging?

Time flies - ah no. Time stays - we go.

Like when you watch a three-hour movie about the Titanic and realize
that the stars look to you like they are teenagers. I prepare you for the
pain.

Or when you find yourself asking people to repeat what they have said
because you did not quite hear them. "Could you repeat that?" "Would
you care to repeat what you said?" "Excuse me, but, huh?"

Recently with our bright young high school ministerial intern we
discussed an upcoming sermon and choices for illustrations. "We could
mention the death of Robert Kennedy...You remember that don't you?"
Well, no. That happened in 1968 and I was born in 1979.

Or, on a more serious note, you begin to feel the onset of age as you
see that the great reforms you had hoped might occur in your own
lifetime lie still buried under heaps of sloth and falsehood and pride.

For example, the bright future of our church lies buried under the
absence of excellent ministers, fine young people to lead our congregations into a new millenium. But do you ever hear our denomination,
ever, speak directly to this potential? A thousand boards and agencies,
ten thousands of meetings, scores of social services, any remarkable
number of revisions in our baptismal theology, a gender rainbowepisco-
pacy, fine international offices, a bilingual hymnal and intricatediscus-
sions of the importance of the cradle roll—all these and more as a church
we could happily stow onto the Titanic. We cannot do without good
leadership, though. Ten years ago I might have thought that message had
a fighting chance in our church. But time flies on, and on. How shall

they hear without a preacher?

Blame some aging for the urge to advise.

As Jesus astonishes his family, a student in the Temple, let us offer our students some hope, some encouragement today.

You can be happy in college, if you will remember six words.

a. Study

An often underrated part of the student life is found in this verb. One reasonable way to find happiness in college is to study. Force yourself. Train yourself. Flog yourself. And when all else fails, talk with a mentor. Find a way to use your time wisely. As George Fox told the Quakers, quoting Hebrews, "Prize your time now you have it, for God is a consuming fire". If possible, work some study time into your schedule every day. The benefits will accrue immediately. Your parents will be pleased. Your grades will be better. You will be happier with yourself. And, you may graduate!

Les nearly failed his way out of Oswego State 30 years ago. He had a wonderful time and made probation mid-way through the fall semester. Then he met Diane, bowling. They had such fun. It made all his other revelries pale. Friendship and humour and love and joy - and she was a good bowler too. After a long and late Friday night, Les asked to see her again on Saturday. "Sure", she replied, "we can study together. One night a week of parties is plenty." Les walked home on cloud nine, waiting for tomorrow, certain she was kidding. But 8 pm Saturday night came and Les walked along Lake Ontario toward the dorm. He was dressed for the evening, but Diane met him at the door in jeans with a stack of books. So Les went to the library for the first time that semester. He squeeked by the fall and spring, picked up speed and graduated with his class. Diane and he were married just before he went off to Princeton seminary. Les will tell you, "I had not realized how big a part of college studying can be, if you let it."

Let the main thing be the main thing.

b. Walk

There is a time to speak, says Ecclesiastes, and a time to be silent Silence is rare in dorms. Students, like Jesus sitting in the temple, are beginning to think on their own, but they need time to do so. One dorm advisor who worked in a 600 student dorm (Delplain Hall) made just one suggestion at orientation: take a walk every day. Thinking is the process of integrating information and insight, experience and judgment. To think you need time and freedom to step back from the 599 others and their stereos. Otherwise the mental muscle will not develop, and you will go too easily with the flow.

Late one night a sophomore knocked at her resident advisor's door. She was the most socially active girl on her hall - soccer, sorority, floor meetings, ski club, marching band and, even, classes. The advisor was at first surprised to hear her whisper: "I'm so lonely here." Fleeing her own becoming person, she had grown weary. At last she stopped and faced her fear. Said her advisor, "You are lonely because, now, you are alone. Stop running from yourself. Every afternoon walk up the hill to the Ag Quad and back. Twenty minutes of pure solitude and you won't feel so lonely." She quoted Pascal about sitting alone, too.

In walking - we have not spoken of prayer yet - you can hear your soul grow and change, remember and foresee. You can overhear what others are too busy or noisy to hear, even the deeper truth of their own lives.

c. *No!*

Here is another underrated word.

But like a river needs banks, a life needs limits. Otherwise the current of Being spills out all over the plain and there is no direction, no force, no power to the river. You just drift and glide. A good life needs boundaries, riverbanks. When parents sandbag, the responsibility lies elsewhere. Amos says we are to hate evil as well as love good. You will define yourself as much by what you oppose as by what you affirm.

Every "no" is an upside down "yes".
If you say no to steady drunkenness it is for the joy of bodily health.
If you say no to racial hatred you point out the path of future peace.
If you say no to $120 sneakers it is an affirmation of things invisible.
If you say no to nuclear arsenals it is too affirm the sacredness of life.
If you say no to flagrant abuse of the gifts of sexuality, you are trying to affirm covenant and integrity and future happiness.
If you say no to a life focused only on obtaining, you make room for enjoyment and love.
Every no hides a yes, and you can be negatively positive.
We all find some happiness by finding our "no's" and sticking to them.

d. *Fun.*

Have some fun along the way.

One depressed junior spoke to his teacher who simply asked him what he liked to do for fun. The list was made. Do you do any of these things regularly. No, I am too busy. The teacher sentenced the junior to a daily game of bridge, two basketball games a week, several monthly movies, and poptarts every morning for breakfast. He sentenced the student too use his own list. All work and no play makes Bob a dull boy.

e. *Explore*

In college and in retirement you have various kinds of freedom to explore.

Try not to explore in ways you will regret, for regret is the forecourt of hell. But explore nonetheless!

Three sorts of exploration make good sense in college.

> One is travel, far and wide, national and international.
> Another is into the past, mainly by reading.
> A third is across cultures.

Geography, history and culture are more open to you now than they may ever be again.

Explore, with the single aim of finding what is good, of integrating this good into your vision of the truth. "Liberal education flourishes when it prepares the way for a discussion of a unified view of nature and man's place in it." (A. Bloom).

f. *Friend.*

Last, not least, open yourself to real friendship.

The friendships formed in these years will last a lifetime if they are well planted and watered. The freedoms and struggles of that first real experience of independence can also provide the nutrients for the growth of real friendships. In friendship, as in love, there is terror and mystery.

Several stages are visible in the growth of a friendship.
Deciding when and how and who leads and follows.
Learning to give up something for another.

Making a really big life mistake.
Talking about making a really big life mistake.
Disagreeing.
Encouraging.
Parting.
Chapters in a book.

Friendships developed now can last a lifetime. One graduate of Smith College in the year 1914 corresponded through the 1980's monthly with her college roommate. Illness and age prevented visits, but the letters still came and went.

Friendships developed now can transform.

The newspaper recently carried the story of Jack Bruen, Colgate basketball coach. Ill but still coaching when the article appeared, Bruen died at 48 last week. We have known his kindness to our children over many summers of basketball camp. Said one former student, "Besides my father, his is the only shoulder I've ever cried on". Read some books in college, but read the human documents too. They will change your life.

For the best of them, through friendship, will recall the spirit of Jesus, whom we affirm, this day, as our transforming friend.

Study. Walk. Say No. Have Fun. Explore. Befriend.

Some ways to be happy in college. And in life. And "in God".

Chapter 8

Listening to Vox Populi: 18 Northeastern (and other) Sayings

(epigram: a concise, clever and often paradoxical statement.^lat. epigramma.^grk. epigraphein).

Some recently uttered, memorable, preachers' comments, heard and recorded and submitted with appreciation for the practiced arts of ministry in the United Methodist Church.

1. "Tolerance is not enough. What mom wants to hear her son say, 'Mom they tolerated me in school today'"?

2. "The salvation of the environment depends upon our development of truly exciting cities".

3. "One young father said, after we survived our near death experience in the mountains, 'I did not know how much I loved you until you were almost gone.'"

4. "I've always had one foot outside the parish."

5. "What are you all reading?" (Titles Only: *Life: The Movie; Virtual Faith; Traveling Mercies; The Once and Future Pastor; Wise Teaching; Shadow; God is My Broker; Discontinuity and Hope; Spong: The Church Must Change or Die; East of the Mountains; Turbulent Souls; Evensong; Spiritual Literacy; The Last Word; The End of Christendom; Waking to God's Dream).*

6. "Evangelical Christianity in the North is weak and has run out of steam, so that the only thing that is left in the mission vacuum is all this jabbering about homosexuality. There is no mission in the North."

7. "Whenever I use Cowboy Poetry (eg. Baxter Black) in the sermon, the men cry."

8. "This year I bring you a moment of celebration of the life of my father, a retired United Methodist Minister, who died last week."

9. "Jesse Ventura is the best governor that professional wrestling has ever produced."

10. "Once I served a great church; now I serve a church that was great once."

11. "Methodists think that the farther away you send money, the more Christian you are."

12. "All these thing come by prayer."

13. "There is a charismatic transaction that occurs within a congregation through the appointment of the Pastor. This has nothing to do with individual gifts, but rather with the nature of what is, esssentially, a charismatic office. Hence, the lingering power of past deeds and dreams."

14. "This has been a year of difficult experiences that could have been a lot worse.

15. "The year my brother was dying of cancer he said, 'Now my goal is to meet one new person each day, and to enter into the depth of their lives.'

16. "Our challenge is what to do about applause in worship."

17. "Grace always comes to us from beyond, when our own resources are exhausted.   And grace discovers us precisely in the wilderness-Horeb, Babylon, Transjordan, Cross - not on the mountaintops."

18. "The church is like my grandfather's ax - it's still the same ax 100 years later, it just has a different handle and a different head."

Chapter 9

Vatican II and You: Connecting with Roman Catholicism--!Aggiornamento!

One Lord, One Faith, One Baptism.

A thunderous silence somehow has hidden, this fall, a great anniversary. A celebration that should have already begun. A festival! Yet, I have not heard or read a single word of it. I have heard about a World Series, remarkably involving Cleveland. I have read about a trial of the century. I have seen footage of a million man march. I have even heard excerpts from a Papal visit. And I have watched, again, as our country prepares for another Presidential campaign, with the usual extensive reporting on personality and limited reporting on the financial restructuring that is occurring even as we gather. A deep throat said to Woodward and Bernstein, "if you want to know the story, follow the money." Still good advice. But, of this celebration, I hear nothing. Somebody needs to be throwing a party, a thirty year birthday party, a festival! So, rather than curse the media darkness--a not unenjoyable pastime--I today light one candle, one memory candle.

In the fall of 1965, Pope John the 23rd's great three year meeting came to an end. So much went off-track in the 1960's that we sometimes throw out the baby with the bath water in our generational sifting. We forget people and moments of genuine courage.

One Lord, One faith, One baptism.

John 23, that happy, rotund, gracious, thankful Italian pastor, had an inspiration late one night in 1959. From the corners of the earth, he would gather church leaders, including non-catholics, to meditate on Paul's teaching about "the unity of the spirit in the bond of peace." The Council opened in the autumn 1962 and ended in the autumn 1965.

The Bishop of Rome felt that the time had come for "aggiornamento". A renewal. An updating. Change. (Ooh, how that word makes one shiver.) Times were changing, and the church, he felt, would need to change with them. (My teacher, Robert McAfee Brown, a Presbyterian, attended and wrote the best available summary of the council, *The Ecumenical Revolution.*)

I sometimes--confession is good for the soul--despair that venerable, conserving, religious, beloved institutions can change to serve the present age. That is a cloaked way of saying that I sometimes despair for my beloved church, my Methodist connection, aging, weakening, and shrinking with alacrity. I wonder whether anyone, anyway can ever bring renewal, updating...change (ooh...). But, then I see this birthday candle lit today. I remember R. M. Brown's stories about John 23. I recall that thirty years ago a 700 million member venerable, conservative, religious, beloved church---threw the windows open!

One Lord, One faith, One Baptism. One God and Father of us all who is above all and through all and in all!

Aggiornamento--renewal, updating, change--can even come to big churches, with the right leadership.

What a joy to see windows opened, and saving renewal occur. In therapy, a man has the hurt of 20 years exposed to the healing light of acceptance. A clean wind blows upon his heart. In surgery, a woman has the disease of a decade removed through the light of skilled hands. A clean wind blows upon her body. In work, a man has the opportunity to fail, and does fail, and has his real calling suddenly exposed through the light of grace. A clean wind blows upon his life. In marriage, a couple finally faces the truth: this is not going to work. The anger of so many fitless nights is exposed. A clean wind blows upon their future.

Aggiornamento is real hard, and real good.

John 23 championed principles of change: constant reformation, study of the Bible, collegiality, religious freedom, role of the laity, diversity, ecumenism, dialogue, mission. But here is the good news, from Ephesians, and from the portly Bishop of Rome, 1964: the church can change, and in so doing, can gain its life by losing it.

I'm waiting for an invitation from somebody to attend a party! I hear nothing. Even Rembert Weakland is silent. As Gabriel Vahanian said of those courageous council leaders, "the Catholics have become the real Protestants today."

When we were kids, my sister and I loved to look forward to the birthday parties. On her sixth birthday, July 1962, Cathy learned that the family was planning just a small, private afternoon party. To our surprise, when 3 o'clock came, a couple dozen kids and their parents appeared at our door.

Cathy had gone from door to door in Hamilton, inviting people to her party--and they came! (That was not the last time I had occasion to admire the entrepreneurial skill of my sister.)

So, I invite three guests on my own today. The party should be bigger than anyone apparently has planned on.

a. One Lord

First. With all Christians, we serve one Lord. Aggiornamento today should mean for us, the freedom to serve.

A recent documentary film depicts Mother Teresa visiting the tenderloin, red-light district of San Francisco. Teresa and three other Sisters of Mercy are shown touring one of the houses in this area, which they have bought to use as a haven for battered women. The contractor, who has recently renovated the beautiful 19th century great house, proudly guides the Saint of Calcutta through American opulence. He shows her the great hall, the carpeted rooms, the fine draperies, the posted beds, the ample lighting, the mirrors. He hopes she will admire the repairs to the porcelain in the baths. He has donated some of his labor and is clearly honored to be with this great woman. During the tour, Teresa says nothing, jotting a few notes.

As they return to the front door, the contractor asks Mother Teresa whether she will need anything else. The film focuses on her face, as she gives a quiet response. She thanks him for his work. She compliments the beauty of the house. She expresses admiration for such finery. Then she says: "the mattresses can stay. Everything else must go: the drapes, the mirrors, the beds, everything." The contractor takes notes to undo his handy work, but cannot resist asking the saint at the end: "Mother, Why?" "Because, we are here for people. We cannot let any distraction interfere with our connection to these for whom Christ died. What matters is their healing, their life. We must not let anything get between us. We'll keep the mattresses."

Service can unite where doctrine divides.

b. One Faith

Second, with all Christians we hold one faith. Aggiornamento today should mean for us the freedom to listen to others' journeys.

Last summer we shared a late Sunday dinner, with two very close friends, children of Vatican II, Catholics from the north country. It was a good dinner. Fish, potatoes, sunset, candles, and the quiet rosy warmth of friendship. When dusk comes, what do you have anyway, but your faith and your friends? Over dessert, we talked religion, which often we do. Coffee and dessert came, but the real end of the conversation eluded us. I wanted to know what worship meant for my friend. It was important to me, and maybe for that reason, I at last could hear her response. I had entered that prized moment when one suspends disbelief. What of the mass, the weekly eucharist, the liturgy? "I just feel so thankful", she said. "I go to communion and I just feel so thankful." In a quiet voice, with a full heart, she spoke God's truth.

You know, life is a smorgasbord, and some of us are going hungry. I mean, others, different others, can teach us, show us, help us. But we have to listen.

c. One Baptism

Third, with all Christians we share one Baptism. Aggiornamento for us should mean the freedom to change our minds.

Wisely, someone here will, I hope, raise the opposing questions: "Surely, Bob, you are not recommending the church of Rome. I hope you are not going the way of the Anglo-Catholics. You cannot approve of all of the religious doings of the current Vatican. You must not mistake one moment of Aggiornamento for 20 centuries of religious slavery. What's wrong with you anyway?" Or, more bluntly, in the immortal words of my mother in law: "you are wrong."

The opposing point is well taken. I make my list this way. Four things I cannot accept about our sister church: the sacrifice of the mass, the infallibility of the Pope, the celibacy of the priesthood, and the subordination of women. We have miles to go before we sleep.

Still: *One Lord, One Faith, One Baptism!*

After thirty years, I think the church of John the 23rd still has some things to teach us all. About Christ transforming culture--that is Augustine of Hippo. About feeling thankful. About the physical body, and respect for the body. About the Body of Christ, the church. About moral law.

And so I light a candle today. I am so thankful that I grew up in a time of Aggiornamento--renewal, updating, change. So I was advised by Raymond Brown, S.J., for eleven years was served by a RC secretary, have shared countless weddings and funerals, enjoy the opportunity to teach, still, in a Jesuit school.

New occasions teach new duties, time makes ancient good uncouth, he must upward still and onward, who would keep abreast of truth.

One Lord, One Faith, One Baptism.

Let us pray:
Give us, O Lord,
steadfast hearts which no unworthy thought can drag downward,
unconquered hearts, which no unworthy purpose can wear out,
upright hearts, which no unworthy purpose may tempt aside.
Bestow upon us also, O Lord our God,
Understanding to know you
Diligence to seek you
Wisdom to find you
And a faithfulness that will finally embrace you
Through Jesus Christ our Lord.
(St. Thomas Aquinas)

1

Paul Baumann: "The papal encyclical released in March envisions a deepening, almost Manichaean struggle between "A culture of death" and "a culture of life." He says that our liberal society is myopically concerned with efficiency and increasingly characterized by a war of the powerful against the weak. The Pope attributes an erosion of respect for human life to our exaggerated individualism and to the materialism, hedonism and moral relativism it fosters. He says we have turned a blind eye to the "necessary conformity of the civil law with the moral law." The centerpiece of the Pope's argument is that there are certain objective moral facts that cannot be altered, even by our society's instincts toward moral pluralism, compassion, and majority rule. Societies that allow killing will invariably revert to barbarianism and list toward totalitarianism. We need a variety of moral authorities - the family, the state, the church - to take our way through ambiguous moral terrain. In the emerging struggle against the spiritually stultifying effects of technological society, Protestants and Catholics need to join forces."

2

Affirmation of the Body: of Christ, of the person, at the funeral, at the end of life, at inception. The body needs the body to be the body.

3

 We can give Pope John Paul II the last Word: "You need courage to follow Christ...especially when you recognize that so much of our dominant culture is a culture of flight from God, a culture which displays a not-so-hidden contempt for human life."

Chapter 10

A Word of Hope—A Look "Back" After
Twenty Years
Galatians 5:1, May 1 2020
Robert A. Hill

Looking back over the last twenty years of ministry, it is heartwarming to feel the new freedom that is pulsing through the body of Northeastern United Methodism. By God's grace, our churches and leaders have recovered our joy in faith and our confidence in Christ.

Since the turn of the millenium, we have walked together toward our own "North Star", Jesus Christ, who sets us free. Like Harriet Tubman and others who hiked the underground railroad, walking north, at night, toward freedom ("following the drinking gourd"), we too have kept our eyes lifted due north, walking toward Christ. We remember that "where the Spirit of the Lord is, there is freedom". It has been quite a journey, this night march, for twenty years, due north toward freedom. But look at the ground we have covered! Jesus is our saving, freeing "North Star".

As the century ended, women were finding full voice and place in our pulpits and pews, on the way "north". Remember how we found the freedom, to agree to disagree (agreeably!) about homosexuality, on the way north? Then over a decade we loosened the shackles of excessive, outdated apportioned overhead, and so freed our churches to run again, and move again, and grow again, headed due north. That combined growth in body and frugality of budget opened up the space we needed, in the conferences, to do the one thing needful - to develop leadership. We invested in preventive and physical health care for our leaders. Why, I was trying to explain to a new young DS last week that there was a time when we didn't even have dental care for clergy - hard to believe isn't it!

We focused on continuous education, for lay leadership. We improved our remuneration and housing for clergy. A sense of self-respect returned, and helped us restore our noble preaching tradition, so hobbled for so long. Today in our pulpits, there is weekly fire and consistent excellence, and dependable depth, as our preachers point to the "North Star" of freedom. Through the long night trek since 2000, we learned again that the Bible is, first, a book about freedom, that is to be read and interpreted, first, with "the glorious liberty of the children of God". The Bible is freedom's book, the pulpit is freedom's voice, the connection is freedom's defense. We remembered that, as we walked north.

Yes, I know, we suffered, too. At least in the short run. It cost us to speak of a straight moral life, in a crooked world, especially when we emphasized tithing and hospitality. It cost us to champion children - expensive, expensive. It cost us to make space for gays. I particularly recall the courage of those moderate and conservative men who found a way, back then, in conscience to accept what in conscience they could not easily recommend. It cost us to temper our freedom to abort with a responsible regard for potential life at 23 weeks. I particularly recall the courage of those moderate and liberal women, back then, who helped us learn from our experience. Yes, it hurt us to continue to fund clergy health care and to hold onto a guaranteed appointment, through all those rebuilding years. And it hurt us to keep churches open, to stay present, with the poor - in the mountains and downtown. It hurt to walk into the open space, the northern exposure, of freedom. It hurt us to agree to disagree, when some wanted a killing frost to fall on difference. But "suffering produces endurance and endurance character." We got by, and came through, and walked due north. Thank God for Jesus Christ, our North Star!

Last night, in a clear spring sky, after reading again from Kasemann's old book, *Jesus Means Freedom,* I gazed at Polaris. I thought about those heroes of liberty who had endured their own northern exposure. Jesus in Galilee. Paul in Galatia. Augustine in Hippo. John of the Cross in Segovia. Luther in Wittenberg. Wesley in Bristol. Frederick Douglass in Rochester. John Brown in North Elba. Handsome Lake in Geneva. Susan B. Anthony in Seneca Falls. John Humphrey Noyes in Oneida. Mother Ann Lee in New Lebanon. And then faces of colleagues in the ministry came to mind. Next month I retire, and with the doctor's last not so cheery diagnosis, this will probably be both my last active and last earthly annual conference. I leave happy. I give thanks that in the new millenium, over twenty years, we have walked due north.

We have followed the North Star, Jesus Christ, and we have joy and confidence in ministry, hearts again strangely warmed beneath the night sky: "Warmth! Warmth! Warmth! We are dying of cold, not of darkness. It is not the night that kills, but the frost." (Unamuno).

"Recessional"

If we believe that life has meaning and purpose
And we do
If we believe that the Giver of Life loves us
And we do
If we believe that divine love lasts
And we do
If we believe that justice, mercy, and humility endure
And we do
If we believe that God so loved the world to give God's only Son
And we do
If we believe that Jesus is the transcript in time of God in eter-
nity
And we do
If we believe that all God's children are precious in God's sight
And we do
If we believe grace and forgiveness are the heart of the universe
And we do
If we believe that God has loved us personally
And we do
If we believe in God
And we do

Then we shall trust God over the valley of the shadow of death
And we do
Then we shall trust that love is stronger than death
And we do
Then we shall trust the mysterious promise of resurrection
And we do
Then we shall trust the faith of Christ, relying on faith alone
And we do
Then we shall trust the enduring worth of personality
And we do
Then we shall trust that just deeds, merciful words are never vain
And we do
Then we shall trust the Giver of Life to give eternal life

Ministry (General-leadership)

Dudley, Carl S. *Basic Steps Toward Christian Ministry: Guidelines and Models in Ministry.* Alban Institute, 1991.

Lebacqz, Karen. *Professional Ethics: Power and Paradox.* Nashville: Abingdon Press, 1989.

Mead, Loren B. *The Once and Future Church: Reinventing the Congregation for a New Mission Frontier,* Alban Institute, 1991.

Poling, James N. *The Abuses of Power: A Theological Problem.* Abingdon, 1991.

Raiser, Konrad. *To Be The Church: Challenges and Hopes for a New Millennium.* World Council of Churches, 1997.

Schreiter, Robert J. *Constructing Local Theologies.* Orbis Books, 1985.

Steinke, Peter L. *How Your Church Family Works: Understanding Congregations as Emotional Systems.* Alaban Institute, 1993.

Weems, Lovett H., Jr. *Church Leadership: Vision, Team, Culture, and Integrity.* Abingdon, 1993.

Wiest, Walter E. and Elwyn A. Smith. *Ethics in Ministry.* Minneapolis: Fortress Press, 1990.

Black Church Tradition

Stewart, Carlyle. *African-American Leadership.* Abingdon, 1994.

Women and Gender

Becker, Carol E. *Leading Women: How Church Women Can Avoid Leadership Traps and Negotiate the Gender Maze.* Abingdon, 1996.

Gillespie, Joanne Bowen. *Women Speak:Of God, Congregations and Change.* Trinity Press. 1995.

Nesbitt, Paula D., *Feminization of the Clergy in America: Occupational and Organizational Perspectives.* Oxford, 1997.

Wessinger, Catherine, ed., *Women in Leadership within Religious Communities.*

Winter, Miriam T. et al. *Defecting in Place: Women Claiming Responsibility For Their Own Spiritual Lives.* Crossroads, 1995.

Church & Society

Bass, Dorothy, ed. *Practicing Our Faith: A Way of Life for a Searching People.* Jossey-Bass, 1997.

Niebuhr, H. Richard. *Christ and Culture.* Harper, 1951.

Sample, Tex. *White Soul.*

Practice of Ministry

Ballard, Paul, and John Pritchard *Practical Theology in Action: Christian Thinking in the Service of Church and Society* (London: SPCK, 1996) ISBN 0-281-05012-0.

Gunderson, Gary. *Deeply Woven Roots: Improving the Quality of Life in Your Community* (Minn: Fortress Press, 1997) ISBN 0-8006-3095-5.

Neuger, Christie Cozad, ed. *The Arts of Ministry: Feminist-Womanist Approaches* (Louisville: Westminister John Knox Press, 1996) ISBN 0-664-25593-0.

Preaching & Worship

Best, Ernest. *From Text to Sermon: Responsible Use of the New Testament in Preaching.* Atlanta: John Knox, 1978.

Buttrick, David. *Homiletic: Moves and Structures.* Philadelphia: Fortress, 1988.

Craddock, Fred B. *Overhearing the Gospel: Preaching and Teaching the Faith to Persons Who Have Already Heard.* Nashville: Abingdon, 1978.
——.*Preaching.* Abingdon, 1985.

Davis, Grady. *Design for Preaching.* Philadelphia: Fortress, 1958.

Faber, H. Vanderschoot, E. *The Art of Pastoral Conversation.* (New York: Abingdon, 1965).

Fuller, Reginald. *The Use of the Bible in Preaching.* Philadelphia: Fortress, 1981.

Keck, Leander. *The Bible in the Pulpit.* Nashville: Abingdon, 1978.

Koller, Charles W. *Expository Preaching Without Notes.* Grand Rapids: Baker, 1962.

Long, Thomas. *The Senses of Preaching.* Atlanta: Knox, 1988.
——. *"The Use of Scripture in Contemporary Preaching".* Interpretation 44 (4, 90). 341-352.

Malherbe, A. J. *"Pastoral Care in the Thessalonian Church"*, New Testament Studies, 36 (3, 90), 375-391.

Marty, Martin E. *The Word: People Participating in Preaching.* Philadelphia: Fortress, 1984.

Miller, R. M. *How Shall They Hear Without a Preacher? The Life of Ernest Fremont Tittle.* Chapel Hill: University of North Carolina Press, 1971.

Van Seters, Arthur, ed. *Preaching as a Social Act.* Nashville: Abingdon, 1988.

Willimon, William H. *On a Wild and Windy Mountain.* Nashville: Abingdon, 1984.

Willimon, William H. *Preaching and Leading Worship.* Westminster, 1984.

Audiotape Material

Circuit Rider Sermon Series. Nashville: Abingdon.

Reigner Recording Library. Union Theological Seminary, Virginia.